THRIVE
in 90

PLAN. REFLECT. ACHIEVE

DAILY JOURNAL TO TURN GOALS INTO RESULTS IN 90 DAYS

MB GUSTITUS

979-8-9928296-4-8
979-8-9928296-5-5

First edition 2025

WELCOME TO THE THRIVE IN 90 JOURNAL

Hey there,

First, let me take a moment to say *thank you*. Thank you for showing up, for choosing to invest in yourself, and for taking this important step toward building momentum in your life. The fact that you're here, holding this journal, means you're ready to do the work—not just dream about your goals, but take consistent, intentional action to achieve them. That's something to celebrate because so many people stay stuck in the "someday" mindset. Not you. You're here, and that's powerful.

The THRIVE in 90 Journal is your tool for execution. It's designed to help you stay focused, build momentum, and make meaningful progress over the next 90 days. If you've worked through the THRIVE: Creating Your Life by Design Workbook (or plan to), you've already begun uncovering your goals, clarifying your vision, and defining what truly matters to you. While the workbook helps you dream big and map out the path forward, this journal is where the magic happens—where those big dreams turn into small, consistent steps that lead to real transformation.

This isn't about simply checking off tasks or filling pages. It's about creating real, measurable progress in your life. Together, the workbook and journal give you the clarity, structure, and daily accountability you need to design the life you've envisioned. Let's dive in—you've got this!

I believe in you!

MB

CREATE YOUR
THRIVE IN 90 BLUEPRINT

Instructions :

To create your THRIVE in 90 Blueprint, start by setting ONE big goal for the next 90 days. Then, identify 3 areas of priority to focus on to achieve it, and for each priority, outline 5 specific, measurable, action-based steps.

Example:	**MY ONE BIG GOAL** LOSE 10 POUNDS IN 90 DAYS	
Priority #1 **Nutrition**	**Priority #2** **Physical Activity**	**Priority #3** **Accountability**
5 Strategies : • *Plan and prep meals every Sunday for the week* • *Track daily calories to stay under 1,800 calories per day* • *Include at least 2 servings of vegetables in every meal* • *Limit added sugar intake to no more than 20 grams* • *Drink 8 glasses (64 oz) of water every day*	5 Strategies : • *Walk 10,000 steps every day, using a pedometer or app to track progress* • *Strength train at the gym for 30 minutes, 3 times per week* • *Attend one fitness class (e.g., yoga, cycling) every Wednesday evening* • *Stretch for 10 minutes each morning to improve* • *Track all workouts in a fitness journal or app*	5 Strategies : • *Partner with a friend to check in on progress twice a week* • *Share weekly updates with a coach oraccountability partner* • *Hire a personal trainer for biweekly sessions* • *Use a habit tracker to check off daily tasks (e.g., water, workouts, meals)* • *Treat myself to a non-food reward (like a massage) after losing 5 pounds.*

My Thrive in 90 Blueprint

MY ONE BIG GOAL

why this goal matters to me...

Priority #1	Priority #2	Priority #3
5 Strategies :	5 Strategies :	5 Strategies :

MONTHLY CALENDAR

●●●	Month : _____				●●●	
Monday	**Tuesday**	**Wednesday**	**Thursday**	**Friday**	**Saturday**	**Sunday**

THRIVE ACTION PLAN

90 DAY GOALS

- ○ ....
- ○ ....
- ○ ....
- ○ ....
- ○ ....

MONTHLY PRIORITIES

	✓	✗	➡
	Completed	did not complete	move to next month

- ○ ....
- ○ ....
- ○ ....
- ○ ....
- ○ ....

WEEKLY ACTIONS

WEEK 1 ✓ ✗ ➡	WEEK 2 ✓ ✗ ➡	WEEK 3 ✓ ✗ ➡	WEEK 4 ✓ ✗ ➡

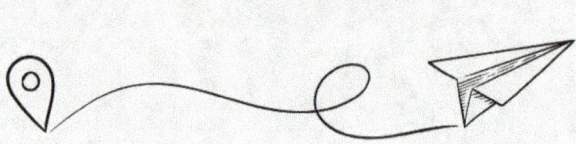

"The journey of a thousand miles begins with a single step."

—Lao Tzu

Date: _____

 *Start your day with intention.*

3 Things I'm Grateful For

1 ....

2 ....

3 ....

My Intention for Today is

....

....

....

....

My 3 Priorities for Today

1 ....

2 ....

3 ....

Thoughts

Date: _____

 *End your day with insight.*

What went well today, and what am I proud of?	What challenges did I face, and what did I learn from them?

Did I live in alignment values today? If not, what can I adjust?	What is ONE thing I will improve tomorrow?

3 Things I'm Grateful For

1 ....

2 ....

3 ....

Thoughts

Date: _____

 *Start your day with intention.*

✋ 3 Things I'm Grateful For

1 ....

2 ....

3 ....

🎯 My Intention for Today is

....

....

....

....

📝 My 3 Priorities for Today

1 ....

2 ....

3 ....

📖 Thoughts

Date: _____

 *End your day with insight.*

What went well today, and what am I proud of?

What challenges did I face, and what did I learn from them?

Did I live in alignment values today? If not, what can I adjust?

What is ONE thing I will improve tomorrow?

3 Things I'm Grateful For

1 ....
2 ....
3 ....

Thoughts

Date: _____

 *Start your day with intention.*

3 Things I'm Grateful For

1. ....
2. ....
3. ....

My Intention for Today is

....

....

....

....

My 3 Priorities for Today

1. ....
2. ....
3. ....

Thoughts

Date: _____

 *End your day with insight.*

What went well today, and what am I proud of?

What challenges did I face, and what did I learn from them?

Did I live in alignment values today? If not, what can I adjust?

What is ONE thing I will improve tomorrow?

3 Things I'm Grateful For

1. ....
2. ....
3. ....

Thoughts

Date: _____

 *Start your day with intention.*

3 Things I'm Grateful For

1. ....
2. ....
3. ....

My Intention for Today is

....

....

....

....

My 3 Priorities for Today

1. ....
2. ....
3. ....

Thoughts

Date: _____

 *End your day with insight.*

What went well today, and what am I proud of?

What challenges did I face, and what did I learn from them?

Did I live in alignment values today? If not, what can I adjust?

What is ONE thing I will improve tomorrow?

3 Things I'm Grateful For

1
2
3

Thoughts

Date: _____

 *Start your day with intention.*

3 Things I'm Grateful For

1 ....

2 ....

3 ....

My Intention for Today is

....

....

....

....

My 3 Priorities for Today

1 ....

2 ....

3 ....

Thoughts

Date: _____

 *End your day with insight.*

What went well today, and what am I proud of?	What challenges did I face, and what did I learn from them?

Did I live in alignment values today? If not, what can I adjust?	What is ONE thing I will improve tomorrow?

3 Things I'm Grateful For

1 ....

2 ....

3 ....

Thoughts

Date: _____

 *Start your day with intention.*

👏 3 Things I'm Grateful For

1 ....

2 ....

3 ....

🎯 My Intention for Today is

....

....

....

....

📝 My 3 Priorities for Today

1 ....

2 ....

3 ....

📖 Thoughts

Date: _____

 *End your day with insight.*

What went well today, and what am I proud of?

What challenges did I face, and what did I learn from them?

Did I live in alignment values today? If not, what can I adjust?

What is ONE thing I will improve tomorrow?

3 Things I'm Grateful For

1 ....

2 ....

3 ....

Thoughts

Date: _____

 *Start your day with intention.*

3 Things I'm Grateful For

1 ....

2 ....

3 ....

My Intention for Today is

....

....

....

....

My 3 Priorities for Today

1 ....

2 ....

3 ....

Thoughts

Date: _____

 *End your day with insight.*

What went well today, and what am I proud of?

What challenges did I face, and what did I learn from them?

Did I live in alignment values today? If not, what can I adjust?

What is ONE thing I will improve tomorrow?

3 Things I'm Grateful For

1. ....
2. ....
3. ....

Thoughts

WEEKLY REVIEW

DATE _____

THINGS THAT WORKED WELL
THIS WEEK

HOW MUCH TIME DID I SPEND ON
QUADRANT 2 ACTIVITIES?

CHANGES I NEED TO MAKE NEXT WEEK

_____

_____

_____

_____

_____

WHERE DID I LET DISTRACTIONS
STEAL MY TIME?

DID I FOCUS ON MY BIG ROCKS?

☆ ☆ ☆ ☆ ☆

"It's not what we do once in a while that shapes our lives, but what we do consistently."

—Tony Robbins

Date: _____

 *Start your day with intention.*

3 Things I'm Grateful For

1
2
3

My Intention for Today is

My 3 Priorities for Today

1
2
3

Thoughts

Date: _____

 *End your day with insight.*

What went well today, and what am I proud of?	What challenges did I face, and what did I learn from them?

Did I live in alignment values today? If not, what can I adjust?	What is ONE thing I will improve tomorrow?

3 Things I'm Grateful For

1 ....

2 ....

3 ....

Thoughts

Date: _____

 *Start your day with intention.*

👏 3 Things I'm Grateful For

1. ....
2. ....
3. ....

🎯 My Intention for Today is

....

....

....

....

📝 My 3 Priorities for Today

1. ....
2. ....
3. ....

📖 Thoughts

Date: _____

 *End your day with insight.*

What went well today, and what am I proud of?

What challenges did I face, and what did I learn from them?

Did I live in alignment values today? If not, what can I adjust?

What is ONE thing I will improve tomorrow?

3 Things I'm Grateful For

1 ....
2 ....
3 ....

Thoughts

Date: _____

 *Start your day with intention.*

3 Things I'm Grateful For

1 ....

2 ....

3 ....

My Intention for Today is

....

....

....

....

My 3 Priorities for Today

1 ....

2 ....

3 ....

Thoughts

Date: _____

 *End your day with insight.*

What went well today, and what am I proud of?

What challenges did I face, and what did I learn from them?

Did I live in alignment values today? If not, what can I adjust?

What is ONE thing I will improve tomorrow?

3 Things I'm Grateful For

1 ....

2 ....

3 ....

Thoughts

Date: _____

 *Start your day with intention.*

👏 3 Things I'm Grateful For

1 ....

2 ....

3 ....

🎯 My Intention for Today is

....

....

....

....

📑 My 3 Priorities for Today

1 ....

2 ....

3 ....

📖 Thoughts

Date: _____

 *End your day with insight.*

What went well today, and what am I proud of?

What challenges did I face, and what did I learn from them?

Did I live in alignment values today? If not, what can I adjust?

What is ONE thing I will improve tomorrow?

3 Things I'm Grateful For

1. ....
2. ....
3. ....

Thoughts

Date: _____

 *Start your day with intention.*

3 Things I'm Grateful For

1 ....

2 ....

3 ....

My Intention for Today is

....

....

....

....

My 3 Priorities for Today

1 ....

2 ....

3 ....

Thoughts

Date: _____

 *End your day with insight.*

What went well today, and what am I proud of?	What challenges did I face, and what did I learn from them?

Did I live in alignment values today? If not, what can I adjust?	What is ONE thing I will improve tomorrow?

3 Things I'm Grateful For

1

2

3

Thoughts

Date: _____

 *Start your day with intention.*

👏 3 Things I'm Grateful For

1. ....
2. ....
3. ....

🎯 My Intention for Today is

....

....

....

....

📑 My 3 Priorities for Today

1. ....
2. ....
3. ....

📖 Thoughts

Date: _____

 *End your day with insight.*

What went well today, and what am I proud of?

What challenges did I face, and what did I learn from them?

Did I live in alignment values today? If not, what can I adjust?

What is ONE thing I will improve tomorrow?

3 Things I'm Grateful For

1 ....

2 ....

3 ....

Thoughts

Date: _____

 *Start your day with intention.*

☀ 3 Things I'm Grateful For

1 ....

2 ....

3 ....

◎ My Intention for Today is

....

....

....

....

My 3 Priorities for Today

1 ....

2 ....

3 ....

📖 Thoughts

Date: _____

 *End your day with insight.*

What went well today, and what am I proud of?	What challenges did I face, and what did I learn from them?

Did I live in alignment values today? If not, what can I adjust?	What is ONE thing I will improve tomorrow?

3 Things I'm Grateful For

1 ....

2 ....

3 ....

Thoughts

WEEKLY REVIEW

DATE _____

THINGS THAT WORKED WELL THIS WEEK

HOW MUCH TIME DID I SPEND ON QUADRANT 2 ACTIVITIES?

CHANGES I NEED TO MAKE NEXT WEEK

_____

_____

_____

_____

_____

WHERE DID I LET DISTRACTIONS STEAL MY TIME?

DID I FOCUS ON MY BIG ROCKS?

☆ ☆ ☆ ☆ ☆

"The best way to predict the future is to create it."

—Peter Drucker

Date: _____

 *Start your day with intention.*

3 Things I'm Grateful For

1 ....

2 ....

3 ....

My Intention for Today is

....

....

....

....

My 3 Priorities for Today

1 ....

2 ....

3 ....

Thoughts

Date: _____

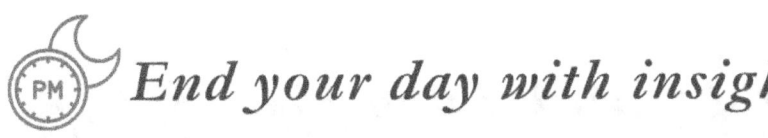 *End your day with insight.*

What went well today, and what am I proud of?	What challenges did I face, and what did I learn from them?

Did I live in alignment values today? If not, what can I adjust?	What is ONE thing I will improve tomorrow?

3 Things I'm Grateful For

1. ....
2. ....
3. ....

Thoughts

Date: _____

 *Start your day with intention.*

3 Things I'm Grateful For

1. ....
2. ....
3. ....

My Intention for Today is

....

....

....

....

My 3 Priorities for Today

1. ....
2. ....
3. ....

Thoughts

Date: _____

 *End your day with insight.*

What went well today, and what am I proud of?	What challenges did I face, and what did I learn from them?

Did I live in alignment values today? If not, what can I adjust?	What is ONE thing I will improve tomorrow?

3 Things I'm Grateful For

1
2
3

Thoughts

Date: _____

 *Start your day with intention.*

☀ 3 Things I'm Grateful For

1 ....

2 ....

3 ....

◎ My Intention for Today is

....

....

....

....

📝 My 3 Priorities for Today

1 ....

2 ....

3 ....

📖 Thoughts

Date: _____

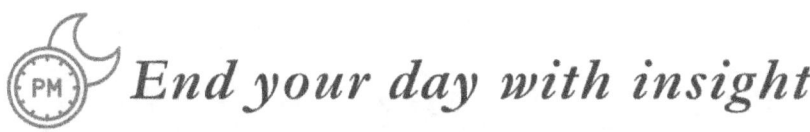

End your day with insight.

What went well today, and what am I proud of?
....
....
....
....

What challenges did I face, and what did I learn from them?
....
....
....
....

Did I live in alignment values today? If not, what can I adjust?
....
....
....
....

What is ONE thing I will improve tomorrow?
....
....
....
....

3 Things I'm Grateful For

1 ....

2 ....

3 ....

Thoughts

Date: _____

Start your day with intention.

3 Things I'm Grateful For

1 ....

2 ....

3 ....

My Intention for Today is

....

....

....

....

My 3 Priorities for Today

1 ....

2 ....

3 ....

Thoughts

Date: _____

 *End your day with insight.*

What went well today, and what am I proud of?

What challenges did I face, and what did I learn from them?

Did I live in alignment values today? If not, what can I adjust?

What is ONE thing I will improve tomorrow?

3 Things I'm Grateful For

1. _____
2. _____
3. _____

Thoughts

Date: _____

Start your day with intention.

3 Things I'm Grateful For

1 ....

2 ....

3 ....

My Intention for Today is

....

....

....

....

My 3 Priorities for Today

1 ....

2 ....

3 ....

Thoughts

Date: _____

 *End your day with insight.*

What went well today, and what am I proud of?	What challenges did I face, and what did I learn from them?

Did I live in alignment values today? If not, what can I adjust?	What is ONE thing I will improve tomorrow?

3 Things I'm Grateful For

1 ....

2 ....

3 ....

Thoughts

Date: _____

 *Start your day with intention.*

👏 3 Things I'm Grateful For
1
2
3

🎯 My Intention for Today is

📝 My 3 Priorities for Today
1
2
3

📖 Thoughts

Date: _____

 *End your day with insight.*

What went well today, and what am I proud of?	What challenges did I face, and what did I learn from them?

Did I live in alignment values today? If not, what can I adjust?	What is ONE thing I will improve tomorrow?

3 Things I'm Grateful For

1 ....

2 ....

3 ....

Thoughts

Date: _____

 *Start your day with intention.*

✦ 3 Things I'm Grateful For

1. ....
2. ....
3. ....

◎ My Intention for Today is

....

....

....

....

📝 My 3 Priorities for Today

1. ....
2. ....
3. ....

📖 Thoughts

Date: _____

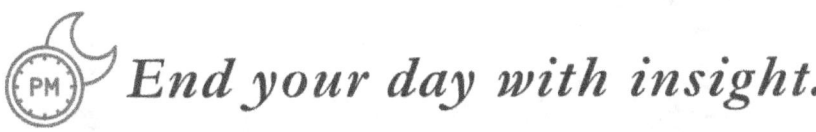 *End your day with insight.*

What went well today, and what am I proud of?	What challenges did I face, and what did I learn from them?

Did I live in alignment values today? If not, what can I adjust?	What is ONE thing I will improve tomorrow?

3 Things I'm Grateful For

1 ....

2 ....

3 ....

Thoughts

WEEKLY REVIEW

DATE _____

THINGS THAT WORKED WELL
THIS WEEK

HOW MUCH TIME DID I SPEND ON
QUADRANT 2 ACTIVITIES?

CHANGES I NEED TO MAKE NEXT WEEK

_____

_____

_____

_____

_____

WHERE DID I LET DISTRACTIONS
STEAL MY TIME?

DID I FOCUS ON MY BIG ROCKS?

☆ ☆ ☆ ☆ ☆

"Success is not final, failure is not fatal: it is the courage to continue that counts."

—Winston Churchill

Date: _____

 *Start your day with intention.*

☀ 3 Things I'm Grateful For

1 ....

2 ....

3 ....

◎ My Intention for Today is

....

....

....

....

📋 My 3 Priorities for Today

1 ....

2 ....

3 ....

📖 Thoughts

Date: _____

 *End your day with insight.*

What went well today, and what am I proud of?
....
....
....
....

What challenges did I face, and what did I learn from them?
....
....
....
....

Did I live in alignment values today? If not, what can I adjust?
....
....
....
....

What is ONE thing I will improve tomorrow?
....
....
....
....

3 Things I'm Grateful For

1 ....
2 ....
3 ....

Thoughts

Date: _____

 *Start your day with intention.*

3 Things I'm Grateful For

1 ....

2 ....

3 ....

My Intention for Today is

....

....

....

....

My 3 Priorities for Today

1 ....

2 ....

3 ....

Thoughts

Date: _____

 *End your day with insight.*

What went well today, and what am I proud of?

What challenges did I face, and what did I learn from them?

Did I live in alignment values today? If not, what can I adjust?

What is ONE thing I will improve tomorrow?

3 Things I'm Grateful For
1
2
3

Thoughts

Date: _____

 *Start your day with intention.*

3 Things I'm Grateful For

1 ....

2 ....

3 ....

My Intention for Today is

....

....

....

....

My 3 Priorities for Today

1 ....

2 ....

3 ....

Thoughts

Date: _____

 *End your day with insight.*

What went well today, and what am I proud of?	What challenges did I face, and what did I learn from them?

Did I live in alignment values today? If not, what can I adjust?	What is ONE thing I will improve tomorrow?

3 Things I'm Grateful For

1. ....
2. ....
3. ....

Thoughts

Date: _____

 *Start your day with intention.*

3 Things I'm Grateful For

1. ....
2. ....
3. ....

My Intention for Today is

....

....

....

....

My 3 Priorities for Today

1. ....
2. ....
3. ....

Thoughts

Date: _____

 *End your day with insight.*

What went well today, and what am I proud of?

What challenges did I face, and what did I learn from them?

Did I live in alignment values today? If not, what can I adjust?

What is ONE thing I will improve tomorrow?

3 Things I'm Grateful For

1 ....
2 ....
3 ....

Thoughts

Date: _____

 *Start your day with intention.*

3 Things I'm Grateful For

1. ....
2. ....
3. ....

My Intention for Today is

....

....

....

....

My 3 Priorities for Today

1. ....
2. ....
3. ....

Thoughts

Date: _____

 *End your day with insight.*

What went well today, and what am I proud of?	What challenges did I face, and what did I learn from them?

Did I live in alignment values today? If not, what can I adjust?	What is ONE thing I will improve tomorrow?

3 Things I'm Grateful For

1. ....
2. ....
3. ....

Thoughts

Date: _____

 *Start your day with intention.*

3 Things I'm Grateful For

1 ....

2 ....

3 ....

My Intention for Today is

....

....

....

....

My 3 Priorities for Today

1 ....

2 ....

3 ....

Thoughts

Date: _____

 *End your day with insight.*

What went well today, and what am I proud of?	What challenges did I face, and what did I learn from them?

Did I live in alignment values today? If not, what can I adjust?	What is ONE thing I will improve tomorrow?

3 Things I'm Grateful For

1. ....
2. ....
3. ....

Thoughts

Date: _____

 *Start your day with intention.*

3 Things I'm Grateful For

1. ....
2. ....
3. ....

My Intention for Today is

....

....

....

....

My 3 Priorities for Today

1. ....
2. ....
3. ....

Thoughts

Date: _____

 *End your day with insight.*

What went well today, and what am I proud of?	What challenges did I face, and what did I learn from them?

Did I live in alignment values today? If not, what can I adjust?	What is ONE thing I will improve tomorrow?

3 Things I'm Grateful For

1 ....

2 ....

3 ....

Thoughts

WEEKLY REVIEW

DATE _____

THINGS THAT WORKED WELL
THIS WEEK

HOW MUCH TIME DID I SPEND ON
QUADRANT 2 ACTIVITIES?

CHANGES I NEED TO MAKE NEXT WEEK

_____

_____

_____

_____

_____

WHERE DID I LET DISTRACTIONS
STEAL MY TIME?

DID I FOCUS ON MY BIG ROCKS?

☆ ☆ ☆ ☆ ☆

WINS THIS MONTH

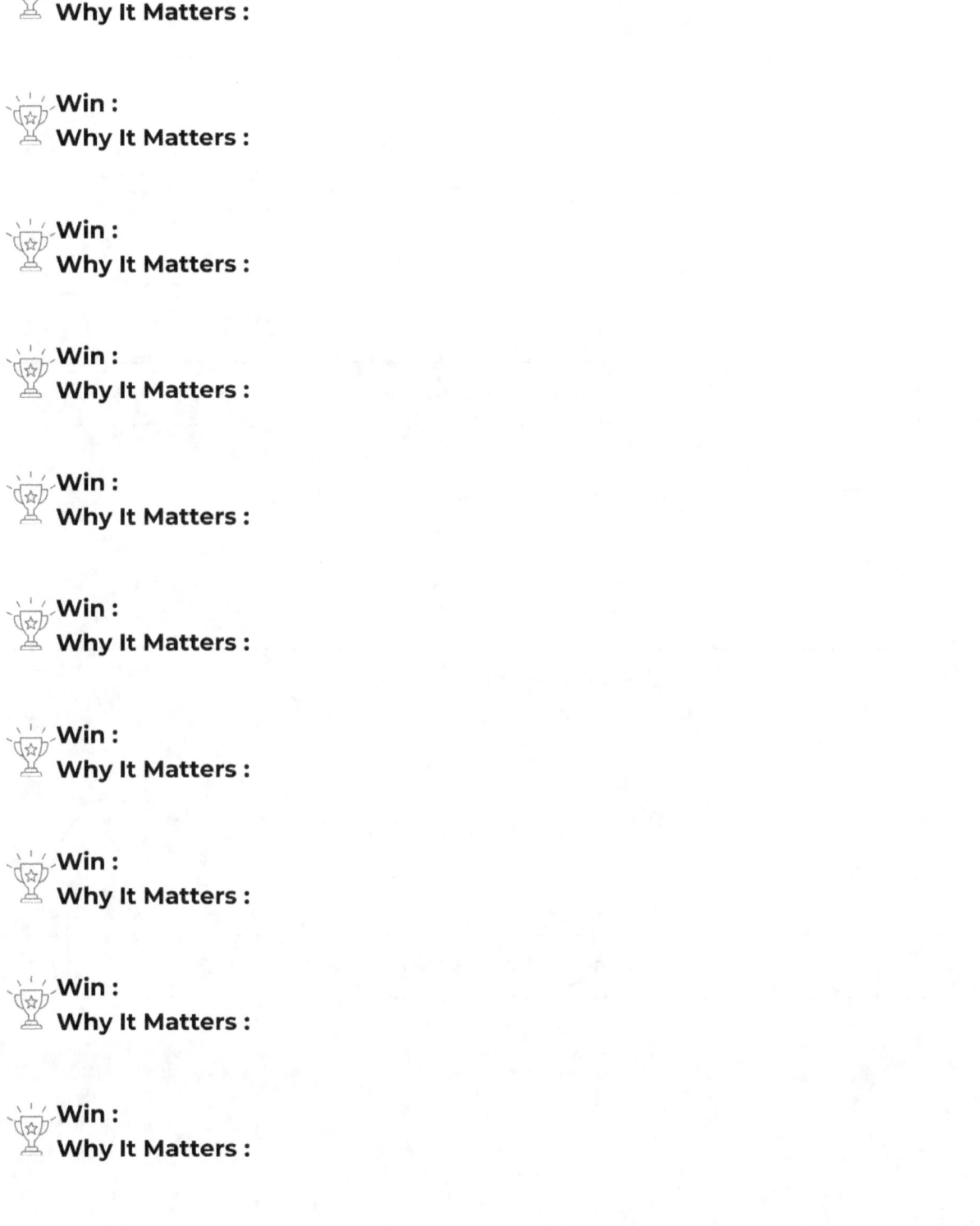

Win :
Why It Matters :

Win :
Why It Matters :

Win :
Why It Matters :

Win :
Why It Matters :

Win :
Why It Matters :

Win :
Why It Matters :

Win :
Why It Matters :

Win :
Why It Matters :

Win :
Why It Matters :

Win :
Why It Matters :

CHECK-IN & RESET

What's still working?

What's no longer serving me?

What new goals feel aligned?

MONTHLY CALENDAR

| | | | **Month :** | | | |

Monday	Tuesday	Wednesday	Thursday	Friday	Saturday	Sunday

THRIVE ACTION PLAN

90 DAY GOALS

- ○
- ○
- ○
- ○
- ○

MONTHLY PRIORITIES

- ○
- ○
- ○
- ○
- ○

✓ Completed ✗ did not complete → move to next month

WEEKLY ACTIONS

WEEK 1 ✓✗→	WEEK 2 ✓✗→	WEEK 3 ✓✗→	WEEK 4 ✓✗→

"Your life does not get better by chance, it gets better by change."

—Jim Rohn

Date: _____

 *Start your day with intention.*

3 Things I'm Grateful For

1 ....

2 ....

3 ....

My Intention for Today is

....

....

....

....

My 3 Priorities for Today

1 ....

2 ....

3 ....

Thoughts

Date: _____

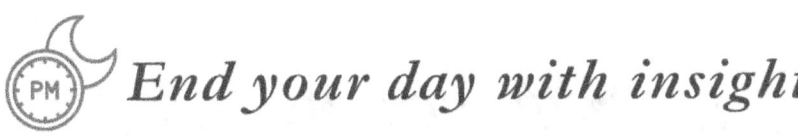

End your day with insight.

What went well today, and what am I proud of?

What challenges did I face, and what did I learn from them?

Did I live in alignment values today? If not, what can I adjust?

What is ONE thing I will improve tomorrow?

3 Things I'm Grateful For

1. ....
2. ....
3. ....

Thoughts

Date: _____

 *Start your day with intention.*

3 Things I'm Grateful For

1. ....
2. ....
3. ....

My Intention for Today is

....

....

....

....

My 3 Priorities for Today

1. ....
2. ....
3. ....

Thoughts

Date: _____

 *End your day with insight.*

What went well today, and what am I proud of?

What challenges did I face, and what did I learn from them?

Did I live in alignment values today? If not, what can I adjust?

What is ONE thing I will improve tomorrow?

3 Things I'm Grateful For

1.
2.
3.

Thoughts

Date: _____

 *Start your day with intention.*

3 Things I'm Grateful For

1 ....

2 ....

3 ....

My Intention for Today is

....

....

....

....

My 3 Priorities for Today

1 ....

2 ....

3 ....

Thoughts

Date: _____

 *End your day with insight.*

| What went well today, and what am I proud of? | What challenges did I face, and what did I learn from them? |

| Did I live in alignment values today? If not, what can I adjust? | What is ONE thing I will improve tomorrow? |

3 Things I'm Grateful For

1 ....
2 ....
3 ....

Thoughts

Date: _____

 *Start your day with intention.*

3 Things I'm Grateful For

1
2
3

My Intention for Today is

My 3 Priorities for Today

1
2
3

Thoughts

Date: _____

 *End your day with insight.*

What went well today, and what am I proud of?	What challenges did I face, and what did I learn from them?

Did I live in alignment values today? If not, what can I adjust?	What is ONE thing I will improve tomorrow?

3 Things I'm Grateful For

1. ....
2. ....
3. ....

Thoughts

Date: _____

 *Start your day with intention.*

3 Things I'm Grateful For

1. ....

2. ....

3. ....

My Intention for Today is

....

....

....

....

My 3 Priorities for Today

1. ....

2. ....

3. ....

Thoughts

Date: _____

 *End your day with insight.*

What went well today, and what am I proud of?

What challenges did I face, and what did I learn from them?

Did I live in alignment values today? If not, what can I adjust?

What is ONE thing I will improve tomorrow?

3 Things I'm Grateful For

1 ....

2 ....

3 ....

Thoughts

Date: _____

 *Start your day with intention.*

3 Things I'm Grateful For

1 ....

2 ....

3 ....

My Intention for Today is

....

....

....

....

My 3 Priorities for Today

1 ....

2 ....

3 ....

Thoughts

Date: _____

 *End your day with insight.*

What went well today, and what am I proud of?	What challenges did I face, and what did I learn from them?

Did I live in alignment values today? If not, what can I adjust?	What is ONE thing I will improve tomorrow?

3 Things I'm Grateful For

1 ....
2 ....
3 ....

Thoughts

Date: _____

 *Start your day with intention.*

☀ 3 Things I'm Grateful For

1 ....

2 ....

3 ....

◎ My Intention for Today is

....

....

....

....

📑 My 3 Priorities for Today

1 ....

2 ....

3 ....

📖 Thoughts

Date: _____

 *End your day with insight.*

What went well today, and what am I proud of?	What challenges did I face, and what did I learn from them?

Did I live in alignment values today? If not, what can I adjust?	What is ONE thing I will improve tomorrow?

3 Things I'm Grateful For

1 ....

2 ....

3 ....

Thoughts

WEEKLY REVIEW

DATE _____

THINGS THAT WORKED WELL
THIS WEEK

HOW MUCH TIME DID I SPEND ON
QUADRANT 2 ACTIVITIES?

CHANGES I NEED TO MAKE NEXT WEEK

_____

_____

_____

_____

_____

WHERE DID I LET DISTRACTIONS
STEAL MY TIME?

DID I FOCUS ON MY BIG ROCKS?

☆ ☆ ☆ ☆ ☆

"Growth is painful.
Change is painful.
But nothing is as painful
as staying stuck
somewhere you don't belong."

—Mandy Hale

Date: _____

 *Start your day with intention.*

3 Things I'm Grateful For

1 ....

2 ....

3 ....

My Intention for Today is

....

....

....

....

My 3 Priorities for Today

1 ....

2 ....

3 ....

Thoughts

Date: _____

End your day with insight.

What went well today, and what am I proud of?

What challenges did I face, and what did I learn from them?

Did I live in alignment values today? If not, what can I adjust?

What is ONE thing I will improve tomorrow?

3 Things I'm Grateful For

1 ....

2 ....

3 ....

Thoughts

Date: _____

 *Start your day with intention.*

👏 3 Things I'm Grateful For

1. ....
2. ....
3. ....

🎯 My Intention for Today is

....

....

....

....

📝 My 3 Priorities for Today

1. ....
2. ....
3. ....

📖 Thoughts

Date: _____

 *End your day with insight.*

What went well today, and what am I proud of?	What challenges did I face, and what did I learn from them?

Did I live in alignment values today? If not, what can I adjust?	What is ONE thing I will improve tomorrow?

3 Things I'm Grateful For

1 ....

2 ....

3 ....

Thoughts

Date: _____

 *Start your day with intention.*

3 Things I'm Grateful For

1. ....

2. ....

3. ....

My Intention for Today is

....

....

....

....

My 3 Priorities for Today

1. ....

2. ....

3. ....

Thoughts

Date: _____

 *End your day with insight.*

What went well today, and what am I proud of?

What challenges did I face, and what did I learn from them?

Did I live in alignment values today? If not, what can I adjust?

What is ONE thing I will improve tomorrow?

3 Things I'm Grateful For

1.
2.
3.

Thoughts

Date: _____

 *Start your day with intention.*

👏 **3 Things I'm Grateful For**

1 ....

2 ....

3 ....

🎯 **My Intention for Today is**

....

....

....

....

📝 **My 3 Priorities for Today**

1 ....

2 ....

3 ....

📖 **Thoughts**

Date: _____

 *End your day with insight.*

What went well today, and what am I proud of?	What challenges did I face, and what did I learn from them?

Did I live in alignment values today? If not, what can I adjust?	What is ONE thing I will improve tomorrow?

3 Things I'm Grateful For

1 ....

2 ....

3 ....

Thoughts

Date: _____

 *Start your day with intention.*

3 Things I'm Grateful For

1
2
3

My Intention for Today is

My 3 Priorities for Today

1
2
3

Thoughts

Date: _____

 *End your day with insight.*

What went well today, and what am I proud of?	What challenges did I face, and what did I learn from them?

Did I live in alignment values today? If not, what can I adjust?	What is ONE thing I will improve tomorrow?

3 Things I'm Grateful For

1 ....
2 ....
3 ....

Thoughts

Date: _____

 *Start your day with intention.*

3 Things I'm Grateful For

1 ....

2 ....

3 ....

My Intention for Today is

....

....

....

....

My 3 Priorities for Today

1 ....

2 ....

3 ....

Thoughts

Date: _____

 *End your day with insight.*

What went well today, and what am I proud of?

What challenges did I face, and what did I learn from them?

Did I live in alignment values today? If not, what can I adjust?

What is ONE thing I will improve tomorrow?

3 Things I'm Grateful For

1.
2.
3.

Thoughts

Date: _____

 *Start your day with intention.*

3 Things I'm Grateful For

1 ....
2 ....
3 ....

My Intention for Today is

....
....
....
....

My 3 Priorities for Today

1 ....
2 ....
3 ....

Thoughts

Date: _____

 *End your day with insight.*

What went well today, and what am I proud of?

What challenges did I face, and what did I learn from them?

Did I live in alignment values today? If not, what can I adjust?

What is ONE thing I will improve tomorrow?

3 Things I'm Grateful For

1 ....
2 ....
3 ....

Thoughts

WEEKLY REVIEW

DATE _____

THINGS THAT WORKED WELL
THIS WEEK
_____

HOW MUCH TIME DID I SPEND ON
QUADRANT 2 ACTIVITIES?
_____

CHANGES I NEED TO MAKE NEXT WEEK
_____

_____

_____

_____

_____

_____

WHERE DID I LET DISTRACTIONS
STEAL MY TIME?
_____

DID I FOCUS ON MY BIG ROCKS?
_____

☆ ☆ ☆ ☆ ☆

"Success is the sum of small efforts, repeated day in and day out."

—Robert Collier

Date: _____

 *Start your day with intention.*

3 Things I'm Grateful For

1 ....

2 ....

3 ....

My Intention for Today is

....

....

....

....

My 3 Priorities for Today

1 ....

2 ....

3 ....

Thoughts

Date: _____

 *End your day with insight.*

What went well today, and what am I proud of?	What challenges did I face, and what did I learn from them?

Did I live in alignment values today? If not, what can I adjust?	What is ONE thing I will improve tomorrow?

3 Things I'm Grateful For

1. ....
2. ....
3. ....

Thoughts

Date: _____

 *Start your day with intention.*

3 Things I'm Grateful For

1 ....

2 ....

3 ....

My Intention for Today is

....

....

....

....

My 3 Priorities for Today

1 ....

2 ....

3 ....

Thoughts

Date: _____

 *End your day with insight.*

What went well today, and what am I proud of?

What challenges did I face, and what did I learn from them?

Did I live in alignment values today? If not, what can I adjust?

What is ONE thing I will improve tomorrow?

3 Things I'm Grateful For

1. ....
2. ....
3. ....

Thoughts

Date: _____

 *Start your day with intention.*

3 Things I'm Grateful For

1. ....
2. ....
3. ....

My Intention for Today is

....

....

....

....

My 3 Priorities for Today

1. ....
2. ....
3. ....

Thoughts

Date: _____

 *End your day with insight.*

What went well today, and what am I proud of?

What challenges did I face, and what did I learn from them?

Did I live in alignment values today? If not, what can I adjust?

What is ONE thing I will improve tomorrow?

3 Things I'm Grateful For

1 ....

2 ....

3 ....

Thoughts

Date: _____

 *Start your day with intention.*

✋ 3 Things I'm Grateful For

1 ....

2 ....

3 ....

🎯 My Intention for Today is

....

....

....

....

📇 My 3 Priorities for Today

1 ....

2 ....

3 ....

📖 Thoughts

Date: _____

 *End your day with insight.*

What went well today, and what am I proud of?

What challenges did I face, and what did I learn from them?

Did I live in alignment values today? If not, what can I adjust?

What is ONE thing I will improve tomorrow?

3 Things I'm Grateful For

1 ....

2 ....

3 ....

Thoughts

Date: _____

 *Start your day with intention.*

3 Things I'm Grateful For

1
2
3

My Intention for Today is

My 3 Priorities for Today

1
2
3

Thoughts

Date: _____

 *End your day with insight.*

What went well today, and what am I proud of?

What challenges did I face, and what did I learn from them?

Did I live in alignment values today? If not, what can I adjust?

What is ONE thing I will improve tomorrow?

3 Things I'm Grateful For

1 ....
2 ....
3 ....

Thoughts

Date: _____

 *Start your day with intention.*

3 Things I'm Grateful For

1 ....

2 ....

3 ....

My Intention for Today is

....

....

....

....

My 3 Priorities for Today

1 ....

2 ....

3 ....

Thoughts

Date: _____

 *End your day with insight.*

What went well today, and what am I proud of?

What challenges did I face, and what did I learn from them?

Did I live in alignment values today? If not, what can I adjust?

What is ONE thing I will improve tomorrow?

3 Things I'm Grateful For

1 ....

2 ....

3 ....

Thoughts

Date: _____

 *Start your day with intention.*

3 Things I'm Grateful For

1
2
3

My Intention for Today is

My 3 Priorities for Today

1
2
3

Thoughts

Date: _____

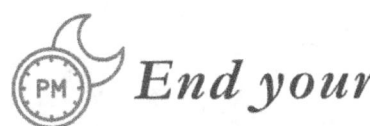 *End your day with insight.*

What went well today, and what am I proud of?

What challenges did I face, and what did I learn from them?

Did I live in alignment values today? If not, what can I adjust?

What is ONE thing I will improve tomorrow?

3 Things I'm Grateful For

1 ....

2 ....

3 ....

Thoughts

WEEKLY REVIEW

DATE _____

THINGS THAT WORKED WELL
THIS WEEK

HOW MUCH TIME DID I SPEND ON
QUADRANT 2 ACTIVITIES?

CHANGES I NEED TO MAKE NEXT WEEK

_____

_____

_____

_____

_____

WHERE DID I LET DISTRACTIONS
STEAL MY TIME?

DID I FOCUS ON MY BIG ROCKS?

☆ ☆ ☆ ☆ ☆

"Small daily improvements are the key to staggering long-term results."

—Robin Sharma

Date: _____

 *Start your day with intention.*

3 Things I'm Grateful For

1.
2.
3.

My Intention for Today is

My 3 Priorities for Today

1.
2.
3.

Thoughts

Date: _____

 *End your day with insight.*

What went well today, and what am I proud of?

What challenges did I face, and what did I learn from them?

Did I live in alignment values today? If not, what can I adjust?

What is ONE thing I will improve tomorrow?

3 Things I'm Grateful For

1 ....
2 ....
3 ....

Thoughts

Date: _____

 *Start your day with intention.*

👏 3 Things I'm Grateful For

1. ....
2. ....
3. ....

🎯 My Intention for Today is

....

....

....

....

🗒 My 3 Priorities for Today

1. ....
2. ....
3. ....

📖 Thoughts

Date: _____

 *End your day with insight.*

What went well today, and what am I proud of?	What challenges did I face, and what did I learn from them?

Did I live in alignment values today? If not, what can I adjust?	What is ONE thing I will improve tomorrow?

3 Things I'm Grateful For

1. ....
2. ....
3. ....

Thoughts

Date: _____

 *Start your day with intention.*

3 Things I'm Grateful For

1
2
3

My Intention for Today is

My 3 Priorities for Today

1
2
3

Thoughts

Date: _____

 *End your day with insight.*

What went well today, and what am I proud of?	What challenges did I face, and what did I learn from them?

Did I live in alignment values today? If not, what can I adjust?	What is ONE thing I will improve tomorrow?

3 Things I'm Grateful For

1
2
3

Thoughts

Date: _____

 *Start your day with intention.*

3 Things I'm Grateful For

1
2
3

My Intention for Today is

My 3 Priorities for Today

1
2
3

Thoughts

Date: _____

 *End your day with insight.*

What went well today, and what am I proud of?	What challenges did I face, and what did I learn from them?

Did I live in alignment values today? If not, what can I adjust?	What is ONE thing I will improve tomorrow?

3 Things I'm Grateful For

1 ....

2 ....

3 ....

Thoughts

Date: _____

 *Start your day with intention.*

3 Things I'm Grateful For

1 ....

2 ....

3 ....

My Intention for Today is

....

....

....

....

My 3 Priorities for Today

1 ....

2 ....

3 ....

Thoughts

Date: _____

 *End your day with insight.*

What went well today, and what am I proud of?

What challenges did I face, and what did I learn from them?

Did I live in alignment values today? If not, what can I adjust?

What is ONE thing I will improve tomorrow?

3 Things I'm Grateful For
1
2
3

Thoughts

Date: _____

 *Start your day with intention.*

3 Things I'm Grateful For

1. ....
2. ....
3. ....

My Intention for Today is

....

....

....

....

My 3 Priorities for Today

1. ....
2. ....
3. ....

Thoughts

Date: _____

 *End your day with insight.*

What went well today, and what am I proud of?

What challenges did I face, and what did I learn from them?

Did I live in alignment values today? If not, what can I adjust?

What is ONE thing I will improve tomorrow?

3 Things I'm Grateful For

1
2
3

Thoughts

Date: _____

 *Start your day with intention.*

3 Things I'm Grateful For

1. ....
2. ....
3. ....

My Intention for Today is

....
....
....
....

My 3 Priorities for Today

1. ....
2. ....
3. ....

Thoughts

Date: _____

 *End your day with insight.*

What went well today, and what am I proud of?	What challenges did I face, and what did I learn from them?

Did I live in alignment values today? If not, what can I adjust?	What is ONE thing I will improve tomorrow?

3 Things I'm Grateful For

1 ....

2 ....

3 ....

Thoughts

WEEKLY REVIEW

DATE _____

THINGS THAT WORKED WELL THIS WEEK

HOW MUCH TIME DID I SPEND ON QUADRANT 2 ACTIVITIES?

CHANGES I NEED TO MAKE NEXT WEEK

_____

_____

_____

_____

_____

WHERE DID I LET DISTRACTIONS STEAL MY TIME?

DID I FOCUS ON MY BIG ROCKS?

☆ ☆ ☆ ☆ ☆

WINS THIS MONTH

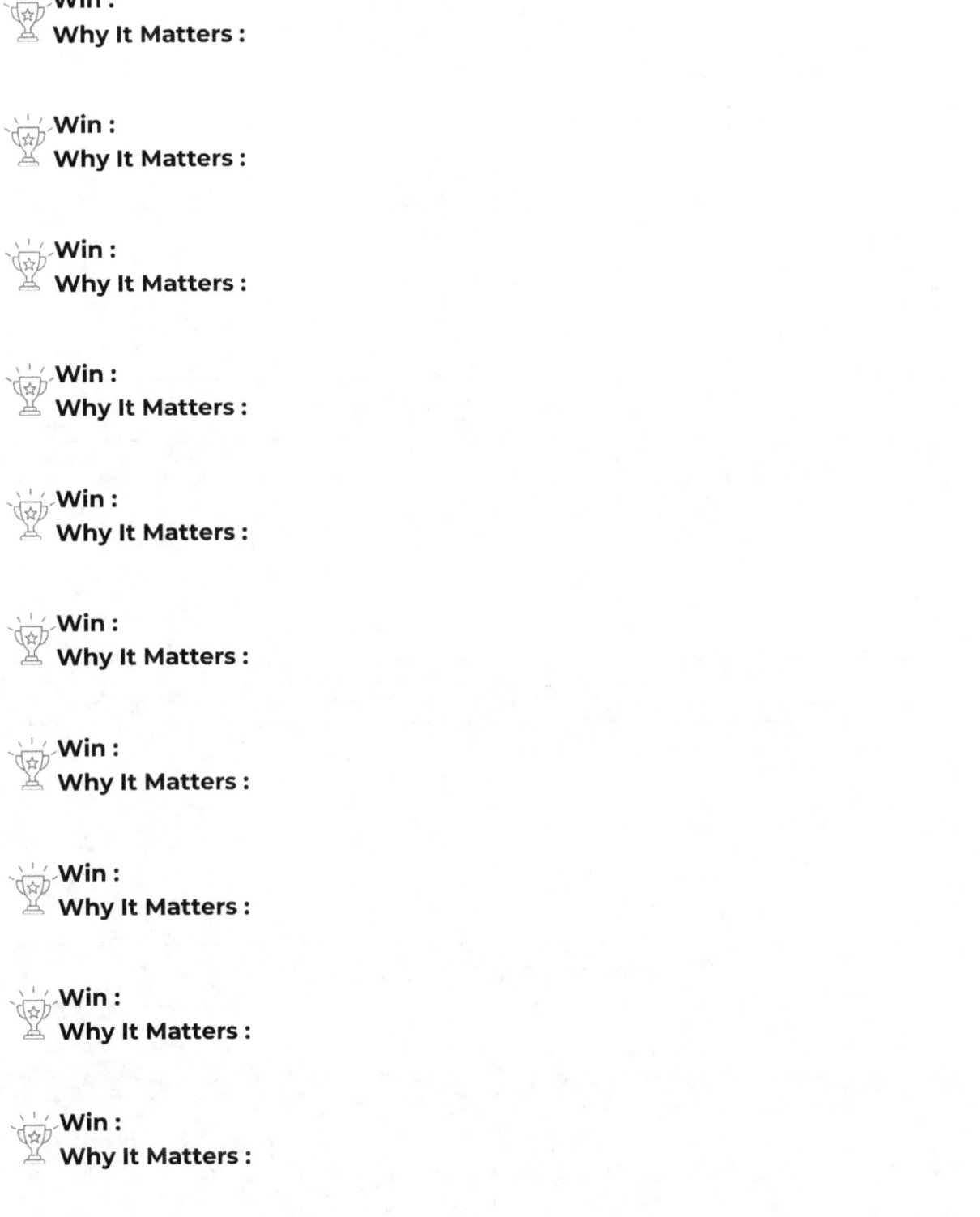

Win :
Why It Matters :

Win :
Why It Matters :

Win :
Why It Matters :

Win :
Why It Matters :

Win :
Why It Matters :

Win :
Why It Matters :

Win :
Why It Matters :

Win :
Why It Matters :

Win :
Why It Matters :

Win :
Why It Matters :

CHECK-IN & RESET

What's still working?

What's no longer serving me?

What new goals feel aligned?

MONTHLY CALENDAR

**Month : ** ....

Monday	Tuesday	Wednesday	Thursday	Friday	Saturday	Sunday

THRIVE ACTION PLAN

90 DAY GOALS

- ○ ....
- ○ ....
- ○ ....
- ○ ....
- ○ ....

MONTHLY PRIORITIES

	✓	✗	➜
	Completed	did not complete	move to next month

- ○ ....
- ○ ....
- ○ ....
- ○ ....
- ○ ....

WEEKLY ACTIONS

WEEK 1 ✓✗➜	WEEK 2 ✓✗➜	WEEK 3 ✓✗➜	WEEK 4 ✓✗➜

"Success is knowing what to say no to, so you can say yes to what truly matters."

—Unknown

Date: _____

Start your day with intention.

3 Things I'm Grateful For

1. ....
2. ....
3. ....

My Intention for Today is

....

....

....

....

My 3 Priorities for Today

1. ....
2. ....
3. ....

Thoughts

Date: _____

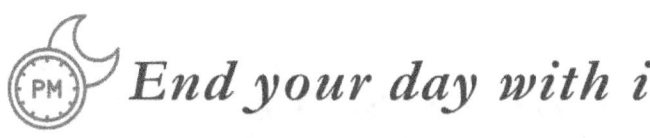 *End your day with insight.*

What went well today, and what am I proud of?	What challenges did I face, and what did I learn from them?

Did I live in alignment values today? If not, what can I adjust?	What is ONE thing I will improve tomorrow?

3 Things I'm Grateful For

1 ....

2 ....

3 ....

Thoughts

Date: _____

 *Start your day with intention.*

👏 3 Things I'm Grateful For

1. ....
2. ....
3. ....

🎯 My Intention for Today is

....

....

....

....

📝 My 3 Priorities for Today

1. ....
2. ....
3. ....

📖 Thoughts

Date: _____

 *End your day with insight.*

What went well today, and what am I proud of?

What challenges did I face, and what did I learn from them?

Did I live in alignment values today? If not, what can I adjust?

What is ONE thing I will improve tomorrow?

3 Things I'm Grateful For

1. ....
2. ....
3. ....

Thoughts

Date: _____

 *Start your day with intention.*

3 Things I'm Grateful For

1
2
3

My Intention for Today is

My 3 Priorities for Today

1
2
3

Thoughts

Date: _____

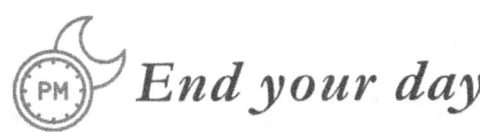 *End your day with insight.*

What went well today, and what am I proud of?	What challenges did I face, and what did I learn from them?

Did I live in alignment values today? If not, what can I adjust?	What is ONE thing I will improve tomorrow?

3 Things I'm Grateful For

1 ....

2 ....

3 ....

Thoughts

Date: _____

 *Start your day with intention.*

3 Things I'm Grateful For

1 ....

2 ....

3 ....

My Intention for Today is

....

....

....

....

My 3 Priorities for Today

1 ....

2 ....

3 ....

Thoughts

Date: _____

 *End your day with insight.*

What went well today, and what am I proud of?

What challenges did I face, and what did I learn from them?

Did I live in alignment values today? If not, what can I adjust?

What is ONE thing I will improve tomorrow?

3 Things I'm Grateful For

1 ....
2 ....
3 ....

Thoughts

Date: _____

 *Start your day with intention.*

👏 3 Things I'm Grateful For

1. ....
2. ....
3. ....

🎯 My Intention for Today is

....

....

....

....

📑 My 3 Priorities for Today

1. ....
2. ....
3. ....

📖 Thoughts

Date: _____

 *End your day with insight.*

What went well today, and what am I proud of?	What challenges did I face, and what did I learn from them?

Did I live in alignment values today? If not, what can I adjust?	What is ONE thing I will improve tomorrow?

3 Things I'm Grateful For

1 ....

2 ....

3 ....

Thoughts

Date: _____

 *Start your day with intention.*

👏 **3 Things I'm Grateful For**

1. ....

2. ....

3. ....

🎯 **My Intention for Today is**

....

....

....

....

📝 **My 3 Priorities for Today**

1. ....

2. ....

3. ....

📖 **Thoughts**

Date: _____

 *End your day with insight.*

What went well today, and what am I proud of?	What challenges did I face, and what did I learn from them?

Did I live in alignment values today? If not, what can I adjust?	What is ONE thing I will improve tomorrow?

3 Things I'm Grateful For

1 ....

2 ....

3 ....

Thoughts

Date: _____

 *Start your day with intention.*

3 Things I'm Grateful For

1. ....
2. ....
3. ....

My Intention for Today is

....
....
....
....

My 3 Priorities for Today

1. ....
2. ....
3. ....

Thoughts

Date: _____

 *End your day with insight.*

What went well today, and what am I proud of?

What challenges did I face, and what did I learn from them?

Did I live in alignment values today? If not, what can I adjust?

What is ONE thing I will improve tomorrow?

3 Things I'm Grateful For

1. ....
2. ....
3. ....

Thoughts

WEEKLY REVIEW

DATE _____

THINGS THAT WORKED WELL
THIS WEEK
_____

HOW MUCH TIME DID I SPEND ON
QUADRANT 2 ACTIVITIES?
_____

CHANGES I NEED TO MAKE NEXT WEEK
_____

_____

_____

_____

_____

_____

WHERE DID I LET DISTRACTIONS
STEAL MY TIME?
_____

DID I FOCUS ON MY BIG ROCKS?
☆ ☆ ☆ ☆ ☆

"You have to decide what your highest priorities are and have the courage—pleasantly, smilingly, unapologetically—to say no to other things. And the way you do that is by having a bigger yes burning inside."

—Stephen Covey

Date: _____

 *Start your day with intention.*

---

3 Things I'm Grateful For

1 ....

2 ....

3 ....

My Intention for Today is

....

....

....

....

My 3 Priorities for Today

1 ....

2 ....

3 ....

Thoughts

Date: _____

 *End your day with insight.*

What went well today, and what am I proud of?	What challenges did I face, and what did I learn from them?

Did I live in alignment values today? If not, what can I adjust?	What is ONE thing I will improve tomorrow?

3 Things I'm Grateful For

1 ....

2 ....

3 ....

Thoughts

Date: _____

 *Start your day with intention.*

3 Things I'm Grateful For

1. ....

2. ....

3. ....

My Intention for Today is

....

....

....

....

My 3 Priorities for Today

1. ....

2. ....

3. ....

Thoughts

Date: _____

 *End your day with insight.*

What went well today, and what am I proud of?

What challenges did I face, and what did I learn from them?

Did I live in alignment values today? If not, what can I adjust?

What is ONE thing I will improve tomorrow?

3 Things I'm Grateful For

1 ....

2 ....

3 ....

Thoughts

Date: _____

 *Start your day with intention.*

3 Things I'm Grateful For

1. ....
2. ....
3. ....

My Intention for Today is

....

....

....

....

My 3 Priorities for Today

1. ....
2. ....
3. ....

Thoughts

Date: _____

 *End your day with insight.*

What went well today, and what am I proud of?	What challenges did I face, and what did I learn from them?

Did I live in alignment values today? If not, what can I adjust?	What is ONE thing I will improve tomorrow?

3 Things I'm Grateful For

1 ....

2 ....

3 ....

Thoughts

Date: _____

 *Start your day with intention.*

👏 3 Things I'm Grateful For

1 ....

2 ....

3 ....

🎯 My Intention for Today is

....

....

....

....

📋 My 3 Priorities for Today

1 ....

2 ....

3 ....

📖 Thoughts

Date: _____

 *End your day with insight.*

What went well today, and what am I proud of?	What challenges did I face, and what did I learn from them?

Did I live in alignment values today? If not, what can I adjust?	What is ONE thing I will improve tomorrow?

3 Things I'm Grateful For

1 ....

2 ....

3 ....

Thoughts

Date: _____

 *Start your day with intention.*

👏 3 Things I'm Grateful For

1. ....
2. ....
3. ....

🎯 My Intention for Today is

....

....

....

....

📋 My 3 Priorities for Today

1. ....
2. ....
3. ....

📖 Thoughts

Date: _____

 *End your day with insight.*

What went well today, and what am I proud of?

What challenges did I face, and what did I learn from them?

Did I live in alignment values today? If not, what can I adjust?

What is ONE thing I will improve tomorrow?

3 Things I'm Grateful For

1 ....

2 ....

3 ....

Thoughts

Date: _____

 *Start your day with intention.*

👏 3 Things I'm Grateful For

1. ....
2. ....
3. ....

🎯 My Intention for Today is

....

....

....

....

📝 My 3 Priorities for Today

1. ....
2. ....
3. ....

📖 Thoughts

Date: _____

 *End your day with insight.*

What went well today, and what am I proud of?	What challenges did I face, and what did I learn from them?

Did I live in alignment values today? If not, what can I adjust?	What is ONE thing I will improve tomorrow?

3 Things I'm Grateful For

1 ....

2 ....

3 ....

Thoughts

Date: _____

 *Start your day with intention.*

3 Things I'm Grateful For

1. ....
2. ....
3. ....

My Intention for Today is

....

....

....

....

My 3 Priorities for Today

1. ....
2. ....
3. ....

Thoughts

Date: _____

 *End your day with insight.*

What went well today, and what am I proud of?	What challenges did I face, and what did I learn from them?

Did I live in alignment values today? If not, what can I adjust?	What is ONE thing I will improve tomorrow?

3 Things I'm Grateful For

1.
2.
3.

Thoughts

WEEKLY REVIEW

DATE _____

THINGS THAT WORKED WELL
THIS WEEK

HOW MUCH TIME DID I SPEND ON
QUADRANT 2 ACTIVITIES?

CHANGES I NEED TO MAKE NEXT WEEK

_____

_____

_____

_____

_____

WHERE DID I LET DISTRACTIONS
STEAL MY TIME?

DID I FOCUS ON MY BIG ROCKS?

☆ ☆ ☆ ☆ ☆

"Discipline is the bridge between goals and accomplishment."

—Jim Rohn

Date: _____

 *Start your day with intention.*

3 Things I'm Grateful For

1 ....

2 ....

3 ....

My Intention for Today is

My 3 Priorities for Today

1 ....

2 ....

3 ....

Thoughts

Date: _____

End your day with insight.

What went well today, and what am I proud of?

What challenges did I face, and what did I learn from them?

Did I live in alignment values today? If not, what can I adjust?

What is ONE thing I will improve tomorrow?

3 Things I'm Grateful For

1 ....
2 ....
3 ....

Thoughts

Date: _____

 *Start your day with intention.*

3 Things I'm Grateful For

1.

2.

3.

My Intention for Today is

My 3 Priorities for Today

1.

2.

3.

Thoughts

Date: _____

 *End your day with insight.*

What went well today, and what am I proud of?

What challenges did I face, and what did I learn from them?

Did I live in alignment values today? If not, what can I adjust?

What is ONE thing I will improve tomorrow?

3 Things I'm Grateful For

1. _____
2. _____
3. _____

Thoughts

Date: _____

 *Start your day with intention.*

3 Things I'm Grateful For

1. ....
2. ....
3. ....

My Intention for Today is

....

....

....

....

My 3 Priorities for Today

1. ....
2. ....
3. ....

Thoughts

Date: _____

 *End your day with insight.*

What went well today, and what am I proud of?	What challenges did I face, and what did I learn from them?

Did I live in alignment values today? If not, what can I adjust?	What is ONE thing I will improve tomorrow?

3 Things I'm Grateful For

1 ....

2 ....

3 ....

Thoughts

Date: _____

 *Start your day with intention.*

3 Things I'm Grateful For

1. ....
2. ....
3. ....

My Intention for Today is

My 3 Priorities for Today

1. ....
2. ....
3. ....

Thoughts

Date: _____

 *End your day with insight.*

What went well today, and what am I proud of?

What challenges did I face, and what did I learn from them?

Did I live in alignment values today? If not, what can I adjust?

What is ONE thing I will improve tomorrow?

3 Things I'm Grateful For

1.
2.
3.

Thoughts

Date: _____

 *Start your day with intention.*

3 Things I'm Grateful For

1. ....
2. ....
3. ....

My Intention for Today is

....

....

....

....

My 3 Priorities for Today

1. ....
2. ....
3. ....

Thoughts

Date: _____

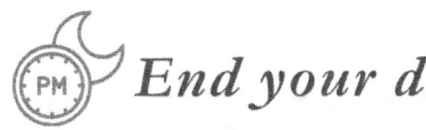 *End your day with insight.*

What went well today, and what am I proud of?

What challenges did I face, and what did I learn from them?

Did I live in alignment values today? If not, what can I adjust?

What is ONE thing I will improve tomorrow?

3 Things I'm Grateful For

1 ....

2 ....

3 ....

Thoughts

Date: _____

 *Start your day with intention.*

3 Things I'm Grateful For

1
2
3

My Intention for Today is

My 3 Priorities for Today

1
2
3

Thoughts

Date: _____

 *End your day with insight.*

What went well today, and what am I proud of?

What challenges did I face, and what did I learn from them?

Did I live in alignment values today? If not, what can I adjust?

What is ONE thing I will improve tomorrow?

3 Things I'm Grateful For

1 ....

2 ....

3 ....

Thoughts

Date: _____

 *Start your day with intention.*

👏 3 Things I'm Grateful For

1. ....
2. ....
3. ....

🎯 My Intention for Today is

....

....

....

....

📝 My 3 Priorities for Today

1. ....
2. ....
3. ....

📖 Thoughts

Date: _____

 *End your day with insight.*

What went well today, and what am I proud of?

What challenges did I face, and what did I learn from them?

Did I live in alignment values today? If not, what can I adjust?

What is ONE thing I will improve tomorrow?

3 Things I'm Grateful For

1 ....

2 ....

3 ....

Thoughts

WEEKLY REVIEW

DATE _____

THINGS THAT WORKED WELL
THIS WEEK

HOW MUCH TIME DID I SPEND ON
QUADRANT 2 ACTIVITIES?

CHANGES I NEED TO MAKE NEXT WEEK

_____

_____

_____

_____

_____

WHERE DID I LET DISTRACTIONS
STEAL MY TIME?

DID I FOCUS ON MY BIG ROCKS?

☆ ☆ ☆ ☆ ☆

"What you focus on expands."

—Tony Robbins

Date: _____

 *Start your day with intention.*

3 Things I'm Grateful For

1 ....

2 ....

3 ....

My Intention for Today is

....

....

....

....

My 3 Priorities for Today

1 ....

2 ....

3 ....

Thoughts

Date: _____

 *End your day with insight.*

What went well today, and what am I proud of?

What challenges did I face, and what did I learn from them?

Did I live in alignment values today? If not, what can I adjust?

What is ONE thing I will improve tomorrow?

3 Things I'm Grateful For

1. ....
2. ....
3. ....

Thoughts

Date: _____

 *Start your day with intention.*

3 Things I'm Grateful For

1. ....
2. ....
3. ....

My Intention for Today is

....

....

....

....

My 3 Priorities for Today

1. ....
2. ....
3. ....

Thoughts

Date: _____

 *End your day with insight.*

What went well today, and what am I proud of?

What challenges did I face, and what did I learn from them?

Did I live in alignment values today? If not, what can I adjust?

What is ONE thing I will improve tomorrow?

3 Things I'm Grateful For
1
2
3

Thoughts

Date: _____

 *Start your day with intention.*

✋ 3 Things I'm Grateful For

1 ....

2 ....

3 ....

🎯 My Intention for Today is

....

....

....

....

📝 My 3 Priorities for Today

1 ....

2 ....

3 ....

📖 Thoughts

Date: _____

 *End your day with insight.*

What went well today, and what am I proud of?

What challenges did I face, and what did I learn from them?

Did I live in alignment values today? If not, what can I adjust?

What is ONE thing I will improve tomorrow?

3 Things I'm Grateful For

1.
2.
3.

Thoughts

Date: _____

 *Start your day with intention.*

✋ 3 Things I'm Grateful For

1 ....

2 ....

3 ....

◎ My Intention for Today is

....

....

....

....

📝 My 3 Priorities for Today

1 ....

2 ....

3 ....

📖 Thoughts

Date: _____

 *End your day with insight.*

What went well today, and what am I proud of?

What challenges did I face, and what did I learn from them?

Did I live in alignment values today? If not, what can I adjust?

What is ONE thing I will improve tomorrow?

3 Things I'm Grateful For

1 ....

2 ....

3 ....

Thoughts

Date: _____

 *Start your day with intention.*

3 Things I'm Grateful For

1.
2.
3.

My Intention for Today is

My 3 Priorities for Today

1.
2.
3.

Thoughts

Date: _____

 *End your day with insight.*

What went well today, and what am I proud of?

What challenges did I face, and what did I learn from them?

Did I live in alignment values today? If not, what can I adjust?

What is ONE thing I will improve tomorrow?

3 Things I'm Grateful For

1 ....

2 ....

3 ....

Thoughts

Date: _____

 *Start your day with intention.*

3 Things I'm Grateful For

1. ....
2. ....
3. ....

My Intention for Today is

....

....

....

....

My 3 Priorities for Today

1. ....
2. ....
3. ....

Thoughts

Date: _____

 *End your day with insight.*

What went well today, and what am I proud of?

What challenges did I face, and what did I learn from them?

Did I live in alignment values today? If not, what can I adjust?

What is ONE thing I will improve tomorrow?

3 Things I'm Grateful For
1
2
3

Thoughts

Date: _____

 *Start your day with intention.*

3 Things I'm Grateful For

1 ....

2 ....

3 ....

My Intention for Today is

....

....

....

....

My 3 Priorities for Today

1 ....

2 ....

3 ....

Thoughts

Date: _____

 *End your day with insight.*

What went well today, and what am I proud of?	What challenges did I face, and what did I learn from them?

Did I live in alignment values today? If not, what can I adjust?	What is ONE thing I will improve tomorrow?

3 Things I'm Grateful For

1.
2.
3.

Thoughts

WEEKLY REVIEW

DATE _____

THINGS THAT WORKED WELL
THIS WEEK

HOW MUCH TIME DID I SPEND ON
QUADRANT 2 ACTIVITIES?

CHANGES I NEED TO MAKE NEXT WEEK

_____

_____

_____

_____

_____

WHERE DID I LET DISTRACTIONS
STEAL MY TIME?

DID I FOCUS ON MY BIG ROCKS?

WINS THIS MONTH

Win :
Why It Matters :

Win :
Why It Matters :

Win :
Why It Matters :

Win :
Why It Matters :

Win :
Why It Matters :

Win :
Why It Matters :

Win :
Why It Matters :

Win :
Why It Matters :

Win :
Why It Matters :

Win :
Why It Matters :

CHECK-IN & RESET

What's still working?

What's no longer serving me?

What new goals feel aligned?

MY 90-DAY TRANSFORMATION

SECTION 1: REFLECT ON ACCOMPLISHMENTS

Looking back on the past 90 days, what are my biggest accomplishments?
Think about personal, professional, emotional, or physical growth. No win is too small!

- ....
- ....
- ....
- ....

SECTION 2: BEFORE & AFTER SNAPSHOT

How did I feel when I started this journey? How do I feel now?

BEFORE	AFTER

SECTION 3: LESSONS LEARNED

What are the most important lessons I've learned during this journey?
How can I apply these lessons moving forward?

- ....
- ....
- ....
- ....

SECTION 4: GRATITUDE & ACKNOWLEDGMENT

What am I most grateful for from this journey?

SECTION 5: VISION FOR THE FUTURE

What's next for me?

Congratulations!

You did it! You showed up, you did the work, and you made it through 90 days of reflection, action, and growth. That's something to be incredibly proud of. Take a moment to truly celebrate how far you've come—not just the wins you've achieved, but the mindset shifts, the courage to start, and the consistency to keep going. This journey wasn't about perfection; it was about progress, and you've proven to yourself that you're capable of creating meaningful change. The clarity and momentum you've built are stepping stones to something even greater. Keep using the tools you've learned here. Stay curious, keep reflecting, and most importantly, keep taking intentional steps toward the life you want to create. Your journey doesn't stop here—it evolves. And I'm so excited to see where it takes you next.

You've got this! Keep Thriving!

MB Gustitus

About the Author

MaryBeth "MB" Gustitus is a no-nonsense, high-energy coach, facilitator, and founder of Mile One Coaching. With over 30 years of experience in leadership and personal development, MB has helped thousands of people get unstuck, gain clarity, and create lives they truly love. Known for blending humor, straight talk, and actionable strategies, MB challenges her clients to stop making excuses and take ownership of their growth—because that's where real transformation begins.

As a Certified Integrative Coach and Master Practitioner of Neuro-Linguistic Programming (NLP), MB's passion lies in empowering others to thrive with intention, confidence, and purpose. When she's not leading retreats, facilitating breakthroughs, or inspiring audiences, you'll find her crafting tools like this journal to help people take meaningful action and design lives that align with their vision.

Her message is simple: Stop settling. Start thriving. And this journal is your starting point. Let's go!

MB Gustitus

UNLEASH YOUR POWER, PURPOSE, AND POTENTIAL